EERIE EXPEDITIONS AROUND THE WORLD

THE GHOSTLY GUIDE TO GETTYSBURG

BY THERESA EMMINIZER

HOT TOPICS

Gareth Stevens PUBLISHING

Please visit our website, www.garethstevens.com. For a free color catalog of all our high-quality books, call toll free 1-800-542-2595 or fax 1-877-542-2596.

Library of Congress Cataloging-in-Publication Data
Names: Emminizer, Theresa, author.
Title: The ghostly guide to Gettysburg / Theresa Emminizer.
Description: Buffalo : Gareth Stevens Publishing, [2024] | Series: Eerie expeditions around the world | Includes index.
Identifiers: LCCN 2023031225 (print) | LCCN 2023031226 (ebook) | ISBN 9781538291931 (library binding) | ISBN 9781538291924 (paperback) | ISBN 9781538291948 (ebook)
Subjects: LCSH: Haunted places–Pennsylvania–Gettysburg. | Ghosts–Pennsylvania–Gettysburg National Military Park. | Gettysburg, Battle of, Gettysburg, Pa., 1863–Miscellanea.
Classification: LCC BF1472.U6 E55 2024 (print) | LCC BF1472.U6 (ebook) | DDC 133.109748/42–dc23/eng/20230711
LC record available at https://lccn.loc.gov/2023031225
LC ebook record available at https://lccn.loc.gov/2023031226

First Edition

Published in 2024 by
Gareth Stevens Publishing
2544 Clinton St
Buffalo, NY 14224

Designer: Tanya Dellaccio Keeney
Editor: Theresa Emminizer

Photo credits: Cover (book texture) normallens/Shutterstock.com; cover (leather strap) donatas1205/Shutterstock.com; cover (main) Bob Pool/Shutterstock.com; p. 4 HEakin/Shutterstock.com; p. 5 JEJordan/Shutterstock.com; p. 7 Jon Bilous/Shutterstock.com; p. 9 littlenySTOCK/Shutterstock.com; pp. 11 (both), 13, 25 George Sheldon/Shutterstock.com; p. 12 https://upload.wikimedia.org/wikipedia/commons/8/88/Tillie_Pierce_%281848-1914%29.jpg; pp. 15, 21 (bottom) Rosemarie Mosteller/Shutterstock.com; p. 17 (both) LivCaptures/Shutterstock.com; pp. 19, 21 (top) Walt Bilous/Shutterstock.com; p. 23 Everett Collection/Shutterstock.com; p. 24 https://upload.wikimedia.org/wikipedia/commons/8/8b/Welcome_sign_for_Farnsworth_House_Inn.jpg; p. 27 woodsnorthphoto/Shutterstock.com; p. 29 Nagel Photography/Shutterstock.com; p. 30 OJUP/Shutterstock.com.

Printed in the United States of America

CPSIA compliance information: Batch #CW24GS: For further information contact Gareth Stevens at 1-800-542-2595.

CONTENTS

A HAUNTED CITY

Gettysburg, Pennsylvania, is thought to be one of the most haunted cities in America. Thousands visit each year, hoping to find **proof** of the **paranormal**. But whether or not you believe in ghosts, one thing's certain: a lot of blood was spilled at Gettysburg.

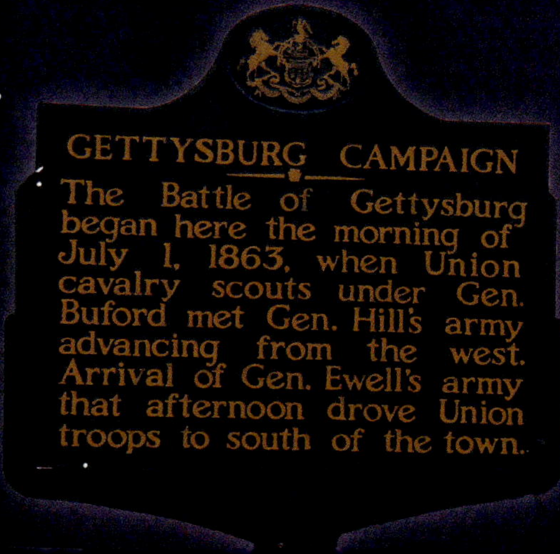

SPOOKY STORIES

VISITORS TO GETTYSBURG CAN TAKE GHOST TOURS OF THE NATIONAL BATTLEFIELD PARK AND OTHER KEY PLACES IN THE CITY. THEY CAN STAY AT SUPPOSEDLY HAUNTED INNS AND HOTELS. WOULD YOU DARE?

THE BLOODIEST BATTLE

The Battle of Gettysburg took place over three long days in July 1863. About 50,000 people lost their lives in the fight. This battle marked a major turning point in the American Civil War. Some believe the dead still haunt the field today.

SPOOKY STORIES

THE CONFEDERATE, OR SOUTHERN, ARMY, LED BY GENERAL ROBERT E. LEE AND THE UNION, OR NORTHERN, ARMY LED BY GENERAL GEORGE MEADE FOUGHT AT GETTYSBURG.

DEVIL'S DEN

Devil's Den is a rocky area on the Gettysburg battlefield. Heavy fighting happened here on the second day of battle. Visitors to Gettysburg have found that their phones and cameras will suddenly stop working at Devil's Den. Sometimes the **batteries** die.

SPOOKY STORIES

SOME VISITORS SAY THEY'VE MET A FRIENDLY YOUNG SOLDIER AT DEVIL'S DEN! THE SOLDIER TALKS TO THE **TOURISTS** AND OFFERS TO TAKE PICTURES WITH THEM. WHEN THE PHOTO IS TAKEN, HE SUDDENLY DISAPPEARS.

THE JENNIE WADE HOUSE

Jennie Wade, age 20, was the only **civilian** to die in the Battle of Gettysburg. Wade was baking in the kitchen when a stray bullet passed through two doors and killed her. A statue of Wade now stands

SPOOKY STORIES

VISITORS TO THE JENNIE WADE HOUSE CLAIM TO HEAR AND FEEL UNSEEN FORCES THERE. JENNY'S GHOST IS THOUGHT TO HAUNT THE BASEMENT, WHERE HER BODY LAY UNTIL THE BATTLE ENDED.

TILLIE PIERCE HOUSE INN

Matilda "Tillie" Pierce was a teenager living in Gettysburg during the battle. She helped care for wounded, or hurt, soldiers and wrote about what she saw and went through. Pierce's house was turned into an inn, which some believe is haunted!

TILLIE PIERCE

SPOOKY STORIES

GUESTS AT THE TILLIE PIERCE HOUSE INN REPORT FEELING AS THOUGH SOMEONE IS SITTING ON THEIR BED AND WATCHING THEM! SOME SAY THEY'VE SEEN THE GHOST OF A SOLDIER WALKING UP AND DOWN THE STAIRS.

LITTLE ROUND TOP

Little Round Top was another area of the Gettysburg battlefield that saw heavy fighting and loss. Parts of the area are also called the "Valley of Death" and the "Slaughter Pen." It's said that so many died here that their bodies covered all the grass.

SPOOKY STORIES

SOME SAY THAT WHILE FILMING THE 1993 MOVIE *GETTYSBURG*, ACTORS WERE VISITED BY THE GHOST OF A UNION SOLDIER AT LITTLE ROUND TOP. THE GHOST GAVE THE ACTORS BULLETS FOR THEIR MUSKETS (GUNS).

SACHS COVERED BRIDGE

Desertion is the act of leaving the military without permission. It's a serious crime for which many have lost their lives. Sachs Covered Bridge is thought to be haunted by the ghosts of three Confederate soldiers who were hanged there for desertion.

SPOOKY STORIES

PEOPLE CROSSING SACHS BRIDGE HAVE CLAIMED TO SEE AND HEAR GHOSTS OF THE DEAD SOLDIERS. SOME SAY THAT MIST, OR FOG, SUDDENLY RISES. OTHERS HEAR GUNFIRE.

THE DANIEL LADY FARM

The Daniel Lady farm was used as a Confederate field hospital during the battle. The house has been preserved, or saved, and the bloodstains can still be seen on its floor. Carvings made by the soldiers can still be seen in the barn.

SPOOKY STORIES

THERE ARE STILL BLOODY FINGERPRINTS ON THE WALLS OF THE LADY FARMHOUSE. SOME BELIEVE THAT THE HOUSE IS HAUNTED BY THE MEN WHO LOST LIMBS (ARMS AND LEGS) OR DIED THERE.

GETTYSBURG COLLEGE

Many at Gettysburg College have claimed to see and hear Civil War ghosts. In 2003, one person said that an elevator in one building passed the floor he picked, taking him to the basement instead. There, he said, he saw a Civil War field hospital, busy and filled with people but soundless!

SPOOKY STORIES

PENNSYLVANIA HALL IS THE OLDEST BUILDING ON CAMPUS AND REALLY WAS USED AS A FIELD HOSPITAL DURING THE BATTLE! COULD THIS GHOST STORY BE TRUE?

GHOSTS ON CAMERA

At least one visitor claims to have captured Gettysburg ghosts on camera! In 2001, Tom Underwood and his family drove through the battlefield after dark. He took a video of what he said were ghost soldiers marching on the field.

SPOOKY STORIES

EXPERTS STUDIED UNDERWOOD'S VIDEOS. IT'S POSSIBLE THAT THE GHOST IMAGES WERE FAKED, BUT IT'S NOT CERTAIN. UNDERWOOD AND HIS VIDEO WERE FEATURED ON THE HISTORY CHANNEL SHOW *MONSTERQUEST*.

FARNSWORTH HOUSE INN

The Farnsworth House was a hideout for Confederate **snipers** during the battle. The shot that killed Jennie Wade may have been fired here! On July 3, Union soldiers stormed the house, killing many people.

SPOOKY STORIES

THE FARNSWORTH HOUSE INN IS NOW A BED AND BREAKFAST, OFFERING **REENACTMENTS**, GHOST WALKS, AND MORE. THE ATTIC FROM WHICH CONFEDERATE SOLDIERS FIRED IS THOUGHT TO BE ESPECIALLY HAUNTED.

THE GETTYSBURG HOTEL

It's said that the ghost of a Civil War nurse named Rachel haunts the Gettysburg Hotel! People say Rachel walks the halls looking for wounded soldiers. Some guests say they've seen Rachel taking clothing from their bags or dressers!

SPOOKY STORIES

HOTEL GUESTS ALSO SAY THEY'VE SEEN A SOLDIER AND LADY DANCING TOGETHER IN THE BALLROOM. PARANORMAL RESEARCHERS SAY THAT THE SOLDIER IS THE GHOST OF A UNION ARMY SOLDIER NAMED JAMES CULBERTSON.

DO YOU BELIEVE?

The Battle of Gettysburg was an American **tragedy**. The death of more than 50,000 people in just three days changed the city forever. Do ghosts haunt this place? What do you think? Would you dare put your beliefs to the test?

SPOOKY STORIES

YOU'VE LEARNED ABOUT THE MOST HAUNTED SPOTS TO SEE IN GETTYSBURG. THOUGH GHOST-HUNTING CAN BE CHILLINGLY FUN, PLEASE BE RESPECTFUL WHEN VISITING THIS SITE WHERE SO MANY GAVE THEIR LIVES.

HAUNTED HISTORY

APRIL 12, 1861	THE AMERICAN CIVIL WAR BEGINS
JULY 1–3, 1863	THE BATTLE OF GETTYSBURG
JULY 3, 1863	JENNIE WADE, THE ONLY CIVILIAN CASUALTY OF THE GETTYSBURG BATTLE, DIES.
NOVEMBER 19, 1863	PRESIDENT ABRAHAM LINCOLN GIVES THE GETTYSBURG ADDRESS AT THE DEDICATION OF THE NATIONAL CEMETERY AT GETTYSBURG.
MAY 9, 1865	THE CIVIL WAR ENDS.
1895	GETTYSBURG NATIONAL MILITARY PARK IS ESTABLISHED, OR CREATED.
1992	THE MOVIE *GETTYSBURG* IS FILMED WITH THOUSANDS OF REENACTORS. SOME CLAIM TO HAVE MET A GHOST AT LITTLE ROUND TOP
2001	TOM UNDERWOOD TAKES A VIDEO OF WHAT HE SAYS ARE GHOST SOLDIERS AT GETTYSBURG.

FOR MORE INFORMATION

BOOKS

Morrison, Marie. *Gettysburg Is Haunted!* New York, NY: Rosen Publishing Group, 2021.

Randolph, Joanne. *Battle at Gettysburg.* New York, NY: PowerKids Press, 2019.

WEBSITES

National Geographic Kids
kids.nationalgeographic.com/history/article/gettysburg
Learn more about the Battle of Gettysburg and why it was so important.

National Park Foundation
www.nationalparks.org/explore/parks/gettysburg-national-military-park
Plan your visit to Gettysburg National Military Park.

Publisher's note to educators and parents: Our editors have carefully reviewed these websites to ensure that they are suitable for students. Many websites change frequently, however, and we cannot guarantee that a site's future contents will continue to meet our high standards of quality and educational value. Be advised that students should be closely supervised whenever they access the internet.

GLOSSARY

battery: A device that turns chemical energy into electricity.

civilian: A person not on active duty in the military.

expert: Someone who knows a great deal about something.

paranormal: Not able to be explained by science.

proof: Evidence, or something that shows the truth of a statement.

reenactment: Repeating events that already happened, often for entertainment.

sniper: A soldier specially trained to shoot well from a hiding place.

tourist: A person who visits places away from home for pleasure.

tragedy: A terrible event.

INDEX